S0-BPO-749

The Freedom Bell

Kenneth Jernigan
Editor

Large Type Edition

A KERNEL BOOK
published by
NATIONAL FEDERATION OF THE BLIND

Table of Contents

Kenneth Jernigan, Executive Director
National Federation of the Blind

EDITOR'S INTRODUCTION

by Kenneth Jernigan

This is the second of the Kernel Books. In introducing it I can do no better than repeat some of the things I said last year when we issued *What Color is the Sun*, the first of the series.

For at least twenty years I have been appearing on radio and television and in the newspapers as the spokesman of the National Federation of the Blind, and lately something has been happening with increasing frequency, something which I probably should have anticipated but didn't. Total strangers keep stopping me on the street or in the supermarket or airport to ask me about blindness. Well, not exactly about blindness as such, but about what it's like to be blind—about the everyday experiences and the ordinary happenings in the lives of blind people. I do the best I can to tell them, but usually neither they nor I have the time for me really to do it right. This book is an attempt to remedy that situation. Even so, I still don't know that I have done it right, but at least it is better than a hurried attempt in a supermarket.

The persons who appear in the pages of the book are people that I know—friends, former students, colleagues in the National Federation of the Blind. Mostly they tell their own stories—stories of ordinary men and women, who think about last night's dinner, today's taxes, and tomorrow's hopes and dreams. These are people I think you would like to know, so I am introducing them to you. And I am also telling you a little about myself. When you have finished reading these personal accounts and reminiscences I hope you will have a better picture of what it is like to be blind and how blind people feel. Mostly we feel just about the same way you do.

Kenneth Jernigan
Baltimore, Maryland
1992

Large type computers also help visually impaired people.

WHY LARGE TYPE

The type size used in this book is 14 Point for two important reasons: One, because typesetting of 14 Point or larger complies with federal standards for the printing of materials for visually impaired readers, and we wanted to show you exactly what type size is necessary for people with limited sight.

The second reason is because many of our friends and supporters have asked us to print our paperback books in 14 Point type so they too can easily read them. Many people with limited sight do not use Braille. We hope that by printing this book in a larger type than customary, many more people will be able to enjoy these heartwarming and inspirational stories.

Kenneth Jernigan taking his turn with the dustmop—equality means equality whatever the task.

COMPETING ON TERMS OF EQUALITY

by Kenneth Jernigan

At one time in my life I sold life insurance—a most interesting occupation. I had a big rate book in print. I could not always afford to hire somebody to go with me and read it for me. I was trying to make a living, not be an executive. I couldn't put it into Braille. I didn't have enough reader time for that and even if I had, it would have meant carrying around volumes. So that wouldn't have been practical.

I had another problem: The company kept changing the rate book as new policies and procedures came along. So what was I to do?

I could have asked my prospective customers to look up the information I needed, but that wouldn't have worked because the book contained information I didn't want them to have. I wasn't trying to hoodwink them. But if you're a wholesaler, you don't ask your customers to look in the manufacturer's catalog and see what kind of markup you make. It isn't good psychology. Besides, most of my clients would not efficiently have been able to find what I wanted. But what would have been even worse was that it would have destroyed their confidence in me. They wouldn't have believed that I was competent to handle their insurance business if I had done it that way.

I either had to figure this out or stop selling insurance. By the way, when I'd tried to get the insurance job, the first company had said they wouldn't hire me but would let me sell in the name of another established agent and split commissions with him if I wanted to. I said no, I didn't think I'd do that. Then, I went off and found a company that would put me on.

So I tried to discover if there was any way to figure out shortcuts to work with the rate book, a formula. I learned that if I knew the annual premium on a policy, the semiannual premium (if a client preferred to pay it that way) would be 51 percent. The quarterly was 26 percent, and the monthly premium was 10 percent. So right there I saved myself lots of columns. It isn't very hard to figure out 51 percent of something, or 26 percent, or 10 percent. Ten percent is easy—all you have to do is move a decimal.

Then, I started on the other end of it, the hard part. I learned that if I knew what an individual of a given age would be charged for a particular policy, there was a formula by which I could determine what that particular policy would cost an individual of any age.

I arbitrarily took age 26, and (knowing the premium on an ordinary life insurance policy for a person of that age) I could figure the semiannual, quarterly, or monthly premium for a person of 50, 60, or any other age. Since we mostly sold fifteen or twenty kinds of policies (there were a few exotic things, but they were not ordinarily sold), I could put all the information I needed (name of policy and annual premium for age 26) on a Braille card or two and put them in my pocket so nobody would even know I was looking at them.

It occurred to me that my competitors might also have such data available. Rate books are rate books. So I thought, "If ours are like that, I wonder what theirs are like." So I lured some of my competitors out to my house to sell me insurance and deduced a number of things about their policies—unraveled the formula and found that they worked.

One lonesome, rainy night I went to see a fellow who was quite well-to-do, a man who could buy (and intended to buy) a relatively large life insurance policy. It was going to make somebody a whopping good commission. There are always fewer things than there are people wanting them, and in this case a lot of us wanted his insurance business—but only one of us was going to get it. And it didn't matter whether you explained it, or called yourself blind, or said, "I can tell you why I didn't do it." Only one thing counted: did you or didn't you? That was the test.

So I went over to see him, and he said he'd been thinking about buying this insurance. I said, "Well, if you do, it will cost you this amount."

Suppose, he said, I decided I want to pay it on a semi-annual, twice-a-year, basis?

You could do that, I said, and if you did, it would cost you this amount.

I've considered buying from this other company, he said.

Well, I answered, they're a good company, and if you buy the policy from them, it will cost you this. And I went on to tell him as honestly as I could the advantages and disadvantages of the other company's policy and of mine.

Then, he said, I'm going to give you my insurance business, because I think you know what you're doing. I had a fellow out here the other night who didn't know a thing. Every time I asked him any question he had to look it up in that little book he had.

Now, I'm as lazy as anybody else. We all have a tendency to that, and there's nothing wrong with being lazy if you properly understand that it means extracting as much as you can for the labor you exert. That's perfectly proper. It's just that a lot of people don't know how to be lazy. If you'll work hard up front, it will allow you more time to do whatever it is you want to do, and you can do it more effectively, and have more time left over to do something else.

If I had had sight, the chances are I never would have been motivated to have hunted up all that stuff and reasoned it out. But once I did, it proved to be a tremendous advantage and an asset. Yet a lot of people would have told me that I was handicapped in selling insurance because I was blind and couldn't read my rate book. And they would have been right—unless I did something about it.

I also did a stint teaching school. I taught in a school for the blind, in a day when blind teachers were not highly regarded. The question was: Could I carry my own weight, and (specifically) could I keep discipline? I figured out some methods that worked for me.

At the beginning of the first class I made a speech to the students. I said to them, "We are entering on a new relationship." (That sounds nice and bureaucratic, doesn't it?) "We're entering on a new relationship, and we can live at peace, or we can engage in war. If we engage in a peaceful relationship, all of us can live happily. On the other hand, if you choose to go to war with me, I have certain advantages that you do not possess. You may have some that I don't possess—and some that I haven't thought of. But let me tell you what mine are.

"I can give you assignments, or not. I can assign things to you in a minute or two that will give you a great deal of trouble, either to do or find ways of avoiding doing. One day (whether you now know it or not) it will help you if you have nice recommendations written on your reports from me—not a lot, but it will help some.

"But beyond that, if you try to engage in conflict with me, there are times when you will succeed in putting things over on me, because all of the brains didn't come here when I got here. So you'll win sometimes. But on the other side of that is this: All of the brains didn't come here when you came, so you'll lose sometimes, and I will catch you. It remains to be seen, then, whether or not I can make it desirable for you to try to live in peace with me. I choose peace if I can have it, but I will engage in war if I must." I made them that speech and passed on.

I had a student named Johnny Lindenfellow, who was at that time in the seventh or eighth grade. He took every occasion to be as mangy as he knew how, and he was an expert at it.

I tried to reason with him; I tried to be good to him; I pleaded with him about the good of the school and humanity; I talked with him about living and letting live. But nothing worked. There was no getting along with him. Nothing made any difference. In fact, whenever I would lay some punishment on him, he seemed to glory in it as being proof that he was a tough customer.

So I changed tactics. One day when he had done something I didn't like, I said, "Johnny, you will please stay after class."

I could feel him expand with pleasure. He knew I wasn't allowed to kill him, that there was some limit as to what I could do.

After class, when we were alone, I said, "Johnny, it's been a long conflict between you and me, and I want to tell you now what I'm going to do. As you know, I teach other English classes in this school. In about two hours I'm going to be teaching an English class, and I'm going to provoke an incident in that class so that somebody misbehaves.

"It's not difficult to think up some way to get it done. Then, I will say to the student who misbehaves, 'Why can't you be a *good little boy* like Johnny Lindenfellow?' I will do that over and over and over until I make you the most hated boy in this school. You will fight fifty times every day. I will call you a *good little boy* to every class I have until the day comes that they will beat you to death. You will fight all of the time."

"You wouldn't do that to me," he protested.

"Oh, but I would!" I said. "It's clear that I can think it up... I did; I've already told you about it. And I *will* do it."

He said, "Look, I'd like to get along."

"So would I," I said. "I'm perfectly willing to have it either way, peace or war. You have declared psychological war on me, and I'm no longer prepared to be passive about it. I'm going to pull out all the stops and go to war with you now."

"Look, I want to get along," he reiterated.

"Fine," I said, and he and I became the best of friends and had no more trouble.

That is one way you can maintain discipline. It didn't hurt him. It probably helped him. It certainly helped me.

I discovered another very effective technique, which is translatable beyond school. One day I found a student engaging in an infraction of the rules. I said nothing about it until the next day. Then, in the middle of the class period, I interrupted what I was saying and remarked: "Yesterday, Frances, you violated this rule (and I specified). Your punishment is this." Without another word I returned to the discussion.

Nobody said much, but I could hear people thinking about it. In a day or two I caught somebody else doing something, and didn't mention that for two days. The next time I let it go three days—then, a week—then, two weeks—and then, three. Thus, the culprit never knew whether he or she had been detected in crime, and the agony of the suspense cut down on the pleasure considerably.

The students never knew whether they had been caught—or when the ax would fall. A lot of times teachers forget that they were once students themselves, and they don't put any ingenuity into the psychological warfare which some students take joy in waging and always win.

We had a rule in my class. If anybody brought anything in and left it there and I found it, that individual had to sit down and punch out a whole sheet of full Braille cells, using a dull stylus and an old slate that wasn't in good alignment. The work had to be done in my presence so that I knew the individual had done it. That was also the rule if a person didn't bring whatever was supposed to be brought to class—book, paper, or whatever.

Once when I was keeping library, the president of the senior class brought me a written book report. I got called away from the library desk. When I left at the end of the period, I forgot to take the report with me. The next day when he came to my English class, the student walked up to my desk and handed the report to me. He said not a word. He just stood there. He had obviously primed all of his fellow students. Everybody simply sat and waited.

"You've got me dead to rights," I said. "Furthermore, you have done something else. You have stripped away all of the things that might have muddied the water. You didn't come and demand that I do anything. You didn't make me a speech. You just brought the evidence and laid it out. Therefore, today in library I will bring the slate and stylus and come and sit at your table. In your presence I will punch each and every dot and present you with the completed page."

I would like to be able to say that I deliberately planned that piece of drama—that I knowingly planted the book report and calculatedly forgot it in the hope that he would do what he did. But I didn't. I wasn't sharp enough. However, I hope I learned enough from the experience that I would do it next time—assuming, of course, there ever is a next time. It worked wonders. It made the students feel that I was willing to be flexible, that I wasn't stuffy, that I took seriously the rules which I made, and that I was not above the law. It did a lot of positive things, and if I had had the wisdom to think, I would certainly have staged it, just the way it happened. But I didn't. I simply saw the possibilities in the situation and took advantage of them. Somebody has wisely said that luck is where opportunity and preparation meet.

Many of us who are blind could get jobs that we don't get, and we don't simply because we have been told by others that we can't perform, and we have believed it. We have been told that we're geniuses for doing the simplest of routine tasks, and we have taken pride in the so-called "compliment."

Too often we have sold our potential equality for a trifle: If, for instance, it is raining and luggage is to be loaded into a car, which is right in front of a door and easily accessible, almost nobody would think anything of it if a perfectly healthy blind person waited under shelter while a sighted person said, "Just stand here. I'll load the car." It isn't pleasant to get wet, especially if you have on freshly pressed clothes. I know. I've been there. And there is a temptation, if nobody expects you to do whatever it is, to take advantage of it.

It is a matter of having sense enough to know how to behave to get on in the world. If my motive in standing in that doorway is that since only one person is needed to load the car and that there is no point in everybody getting wet, that's fine. But if my motive is to stand and wait because I'm blind, let me not complain the next time I don't get equal treatment when the goodies are being passed out.

I believe that I am capable of competing on terms of real equality with others in jobs. When I have had a problem I don't believe it's because anyone has wanted to be vicious or unkind or mean to me. It has been because people have taken for granted that I can't be expected to do this or that kind of thing. And sometimes I haven't believed I could do things.

I know that before I can convince anybody else, I must convince myself. I must really believe that I can get along as well as others. Unless I believe that, how can I expect other people to believe it? To a great extent, the sighted public will treat me and other blind people like what we believe in our hearts we are.

THE BIRTHDAY PARTY

by Lauren L. Eckery

What happens when a small sighted child is constantly told by her pre-school teachers and the parents of other children that her blind mother and father are not capable of functioning as competently as other parents? How does she resolve the conflict of seeing her mother and father living normal lives on a daily basis and then having others tell her (both by word and act) that it isn't so? These are the issues raised in the following article by Laurie Eckery. Laurie and her daughter Lynden were introduced in What Color is the Sun, *the first Kernel Book, and their story is so compelling that it needs to be continued in this one. Here is how Laurie tells it.*

When my daughter Lynden was two years old, I was pleased with the

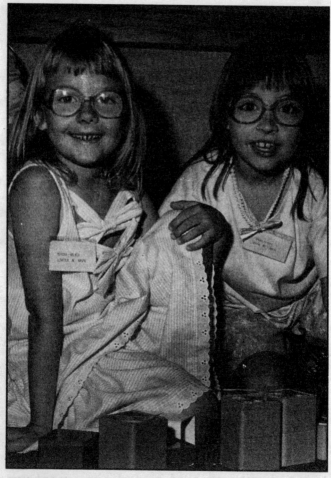

Lynden (right) and her friend play with blocks.

child care setting she was in. Since I spent weekly two-hour sessions at the preschool, the other children had a chance to see me, Lynden's mother, as an ordinary adult who happened to be blind.

The director had become a good friend of mine and was happy to have me at the preschool—not just to sing with the children but also to give them an education about blindness. I trusted that Lynden was in good hands. I trusted a friend who knew and understood about blindness from my example.

When Lynden was two, I did not take her to preschool on a regular basis. If she missed out on some of the activities at school, it was purely due to her sporadic attendance—or was it? She was too young to know or care that the rest of the children, on a certain day, were dressed in western outfits or that the rest of the children had brought paper valentines to pass out—everyone but Lynden. I let it pass; she was too young. I suspected a problem but didn't want to be labeled a "paranoid," and I reasonably expected that Lynden would eventually tell me about special occasions coming up at school. No problem.

Last fall, when Lynden was four and a half and "River City Roundup" was happening all around Omaha, we bought her a western outfit that could double as a Halloween costume. It was pretty enough to be worn anytime. When I asked which day the children would be dressing up for "River City Roundup," the director informed me that she hadn't decided—that she would let me know.

One day Lynden came home in tears. "Mommy, the other kids weared western clothes, and you didn't let me wear mine." I told her that no one had informed me that this was the day for such clothing to be worn. She was angry because she was convinced that

I "should have known." Could she trust me as much after that?

When Valentine's Day rolled around, once again I asked to be informed as to when the children would be exchanging cards. Lynden piped up, "I'll tell you, Mommy." The director assured me that she would tell me.

I bought cards, typed them up, and had them ready in early February. The night before the day, Lynden announced that she would be taking the cards tomorrow. Only because I was beginning to understand that the preschool director, my friend, "was a little scatter-brained" was I able to stay on top of this situation. Still, I was not particularly angry.

In March Lynden had a birthday—her fifth. She wanted to have Amanda, her best friend—the preschool director's soon-to-be adopted child—over for the birthday celebration at Showbiz Pizza Place. We invited her. Three days before the party when we had not been given a definite answer, I made one of the most frightening but also one of the most real phone calls of my life.

The director's reason for not answering the request was that she didn't know if the girls would behave in such a noisy place. She stated in no uncertain terms that the only way that Amanda could come was if they dropped her off at Showbiz and one of them stayed.

Suddenly it was apparent to me that I was expected to be as obedient and as much under her control as the preschool children she supervised each week. I was at a turning point at which I could either choose to back off and say, "That would be fine," or to do as I did.

I asked if they were worried about our blindness. At first there was total denial. When it came down to the details, though, she was afraid to have us walk the children home for fear that Amanda, who was not "trained to obey us like Lynden is," would run off; that she might dart into the street while we waited for the bus, and we wouldn't see it happening; that we might lose the girls on the way from the bus to Showbiz and "How could you keep track of them in that noisy place?"

When I explained, she stated that I was being defensive, not caring about the concerns of other people and risking the children's safety just to make a point. I said that I had a right to "defend" our position, and that she could choose whether that was really behaving defensively or not.

She said that she had no idea that I was so "angry about being blind;" that she had been so proud of me for the way "I handled it with the kids." She eventually stated that she thought Jerry and I should learn our limitations, just as everyone else does, for Lynden's sake if not for our own;

that we were deluding ourselves if we thought we could function as independently as sighted people.

I was horrified to hear her say, "And you know that Lynden is going to know the difference. She's going to understand that she can't have friends over without parental supervision like other children do because of your limitations. She won't be angry about it, because she will understand."

I answered that Lynden would be puzzled and, indeed, angry when other people (teachers, other children's parents, etc.) decide for us that she and/or her blind parents "have to do things differently," when she is going to know from living with us daily for all the years of her childhood that such limitations are unnecessary. She may even begin to think that there is something wrong with her because she's being consistently left out of normal activities.

At length I told her that I thought the whole situation boiled down to a matter of trust, to which she immediately replied, "Laurie, I trust you implicitly!" She explained that she could tell when children came from less than desirable parenting, and that she would hold me up as an example of one of the best parents in the neighborhood; that she was proud of the way that Jerry and I were carefully teaching Lynden, taking her places, keeping her dressed neatly, and so forth, and she knew that we loved her.

It was difficult for me to believe that I really could not trust this "friend," and she could not believe that I thought she did not trust me. I said, "When someone says to me on the one hand that they trust me implicitly but on the other hand will not allow their child to be with us without sighted supervision, something doesn't fit."

My stomach turned at the thought of how I, with my unusual amount of assertiveness, had probably changed the direction of our relationship forever. I would probably lose a good friend; I had "caused" trouble between Lynden and her best friend.

Would I be forced to put Lynden in another preschool? I realized quickly through my panic that the problem wouldn't be solved in this way. It was more likely that this same kind of situation would occur again and again. I could not trust as implicitly as I had trusted previously, but Lynden's education at this preschool had, up to now, been excellent.

But if the director couldn't see blindness for what it really is any more clearly even after observing it, what other "blind spots" might there be in Lynden's education there?

Much as I might have wished for it, there is no such thing as "the perfect school setting" for Lynden or for any other child. I knew, therefore, that I had to solve the problem.

I decided that the next time Lynden is asked to Amanda's, she will be allowed to go only if I or her father goes along. Will the director and her husband squirm? Will they be angry? Time will tell.

We thought things had blown over by the time Lynden enrolled in dance class with several other children. However, on one occasion she was kept from going to dance class because she had a rash. Although we had paid for this class, we were not consulted about this decision. Later Lynden did not inform us of her recital. Neither did the preschool.

The night before the recital, at 9:30 p.m. with no chance for us to invite friends along, the director called us, realizing that "we might not know about it." The children were to have brought a letter home from the dance class. We did not get Lynden's letter.

Thinking that Lynden had accidentally forgotten it, I asked her about the letter. I was informed that the letters had all been taken away from them at preschool and given to the parents later.

We attended the recital, knew very little about Lynden's dancing, and I really began to wonder if I was being deprived because of my blindness. At home I cried about what I had missed.

The next day when I asked Lynden why she didn't tell us more about her dancing, she said, "You can't see."

Suddenly I realized that lately she had begun to play tricks on us and to get very angry. I realized that she was angry about our blindness. She was also feeling that we "missed out" on her dance.

We learn from our mistakes. When I mentioned this last situation to a friend in the National Federation of the Blind, he cleared up my own doubts about my blindness by asking,

"Did you have Lynden show you what she was learning?" No, we had not gotten down on the floor to have her show us.

When I explained to Lynden that we missed out on her dance not because we couldn't see but because we had not asked her to show us what she was doing, she was immediately relieved. She gleefully showed us the entire dance routine, taking on the role of the dance instructor. It was hilarious, entertaining, and enlightening.

Suddenly it appeared that she understood that we could be trusted, that we didn't necessarily not know what was going on just because we can't see. Her general behavior was back to normal.

I know that we will have to deal with other situations similar to these. I know that I must be wiser than to trust even good friends when it comes to dealing with issues of blindness, and I know that I must trust my own knowledge and stand by it.

I know that Lynden will be confused for some time, but I hope that someday she will read what I have written and will be reminded of what she said to me when she was not quite five years old: "Mommy, I wish you could see."

Oh, dear, I thought. Not a pity party from my own kid! "Lynden, what would be different if I could see?" I inquired.

" 'Cause then, Mommy, people wouldn't talk to you like you were a kid."

THE FREEDOM BELL

by Joanne Wilson

"Let freedom ring" is a theme that runs through American Democracy from the founding of the republic to the present day. It has meant many things to many people, but to the staff and students at the Louisiana Center for the Blind it means the chance for a full life—the rights (but also the responsibilities) of first-class citizenship. It means the chance for a job, a home, and the opportunity to give as well as take.

The founder of the Louisiana Center for the Blind is Joanne Wilson. In the mid 1960s she was a student of mine, struggling with the problems of how to function as a blind person. She went on to become a successful elementary school teacher and a wife and mother. Today she is running a center to train the oncoming generation of the blind.

*She learned; she lived what she
learned; and today she is giving to
others, passing on not only her knowledge but also her beliefs and dreams.
Here is what she said at a recent meeting of the National Federation of the
Blind.*

The Louisiana Center for the Blind
gives to each of its students at their
graduation party a plaque, and on the
bottom of that plaque it says, "Together We Are Changing What it
Means to be Blind." All of our students
know that that "together" means the
National Federation of the Blind. It
means what has been done since 1940.
It means the beliefs, the goals, and the
dreams of all of us. They know when
they are in the Center, that it's not
just the staff, and it's not just the
other students or the former student
or the Louisiana chapter. They know
that it is the entire National Federation of the Blind. They know that

Joanne Wilson is the founder and administrator of the Louisiana Center for the Blind.

what they accomplish is in our hopes, our beliefs, and our dreams. When they leave the Louisiana Center for the Blind, they know that there is a whole structure behind them in the form of the National Federation of the Blind. And most importantly, they know that they must give back to that structure. They must give back to the

National Federation of the Blind and pass on the dreams and the beliefs and the opportunities that they have received at the Louisiana Center for the Blind.

The Louisiana Center for the Blind was started on October 1, 1985. We now own our own classroom building and our own apartment complex, which the students live in. We have students now coming to us not only from Louisiana but from seven other states.

We teach cane travel, typing, Braille, home economics—the usual courses that are taught in rehabilitation centers. But beyond all that, we teach genuine belief and hope and high expectations and confidence to our students. We teach them that they truly can change what it means to be blind.

One of the traditions that we have at the Louisiana Center for the Blind is our freedom bell. We have a big old school bell (a hand-rung school bell) that sits up in our Braille room. Throughout our short history, whenever a student calls us with some success or some good news, when something very important happens that affects all of us as blind people, we ring the freedom bell. In the past few months we have rung the bell for George, who called up and said, "I got my first check today from the naval base." We rang the bell when Maria said, "I'm twenty-two years old, but this is the first time I went out and bought a dress for myself."

We rang the bell when John, our young lawyer, came running in. He had graduated from the program: "I haven't called my parents yet. I haven't told my girlfriend yet. I am telling you first. I just got a job as a lawyer."

We rang the bell after two trips down to the state legislature to work on the Braille law. We rang the bell

when we found that the Braille law
indeed got passed. We rang the bell
for Lillian, who received her high
school graduation equivalency di-
ploma, and for the many other
students who received their diplomas.
We rang the bell when Nancy and
John, two of our former students, got
married. We rang the bell when Lina
and Jimmy had their first baby. We
rang the bell for our first play on open-
ing night. We rang our bell when the
first crop came in from our garden,
when we had our first produce as
blind people from our very own garden. We rang the bell when all of our
nervous and scared students got back
from Mardi Gras, an event that they
had been dreading for weeks. They got
through the crowds. They got through
the mobs and proved to themselves inside that they could be successful,
capable individuals.

We rang the bell when Maria was
able to cross Bonner Street, a street

which she was scared to death to cross with a cane. We ring the bell when our college students call in and say, "Hey, I passed a course, and I got a 3.0 average this semester."

We rang the bell when Patty passed her bar exam. She is now working as a public defender in Shreveport. We rang the bell when Barry began managing three restaurants in Shreveport, when A.J. got his vending stand, when Joie got his factory job working for Boeing Aircraft, when Connie got a job as a nurse, and when Yvonda successfully finished business school.

We rang the bell when our students successfully prepared and served a meal for forty. We are about ready to ring it again. One of our students is ready to go back to being an elementary school teacher and another back to being a scientist at Los Alamos National Laboratories in New Mexico. We have another student, who is about ready to graduate and go into child care.

We ring the bell when our students call up and say, "Hey, I was elected president of our local chapter, or vice president," or "I just joined my local chapter." We rang the bell when Zach and Sheena said, "We got Pennsylvania and New Jersey to send us to you. We want good rehabilitation training." We rang the bell when Chris lit her first fire on a camping trip.

These are all times when we rang the freedom bell, but the real truth is what happens to our students. Here, in their own words, is what a few of them have to say.

Zach Shore: My first day at the Center I went into cooking class, and I asked my instructor, "What should I make today?"

She said, "You are going to bake Andrea's birthday cake today." I thought she was insane. I'd never done that before, but she said, "You can do it." It really turned out to be pretty good.

When I got to my cane travel class on my second day, my instructor said, "Zach, I'm sending you out on a route today." He had me on the street on the second day, and a wave of panic came over me. This teacher is obviously a raving lunatic. I didn't think I could do it, but I did. I came back safely, and my travel is getting better. The staff is very good. They really care about us. They really push us to do what we don't think we can do, and we find that we really can.

Tom Ley: I'm currently a senior at Louisiana Tech, majoring in mathematics and physics education. Before attending the Center I had limited myself, simply because I didn't have confidence in myself as a blind person if it involved going into an unfamiliar situation or doing unfamiliar things. After being there for only a month and a half, I could feel the limiting bonds

I had placed upon myself melting away, and my horizons expanding about me. That's a gift I can never repay except by working as hard as I can for the Federation and its goals.

Roland Allen: I completed my training at the Center about a year ago. When I left, I felt that I gained several important things. But the most important thing that I got from the Center was the fact that I have accepted my blindness. When I first went to the Center, I had planned on going to college, and I was real scared to go. I knew that I wouldn't make it with the skills I had. After I left the Center, I felt confident that I could get in there and do what I wanted to.

Cheryl Domingue: I, too, like Zach, when I first arrived at the Center, thought that not only was the cooking instructor insane, but that they all were insane having me do the things they wanted me to do. The thing I thought was more horrifying than anything else was having a blind travel instructor. I thought that was really crazy. But after a few days of being there, and after seeing what all of the other students who had been there for some time had done with themselves, and after I saw how well my blind instructors were doing, I figured if they could all do it, so could I. I didn't have any confidence in myself at all when I came to the Center but now have all the confidence in the world in myself. I am now a college student. I completed my first semester at the Nickel State University with a 3.0 average. Without the support of my family and all the friends I have made in the National Federation of the Blind, and especially my two children (Sheila and Shawn) who are here with me, I could not have made it.

So there you have it. Let the freedom bell ring!

Gardening at the Louisiana Center for the Blind.

BEING BLIND
(My true story)

by Sindy Greenwell

Sindy Greenwell is a fifth grader at Lothian Elementary School in Anne Arundel County, Maryland. She wants to be a writer when she grows up. I believe she has a good start, and I think you'll agree with me.

I was born blind. I could read large print until I was 5. Now I'm 10 and totally blind. I go to a public school. Being blind requires a 10-pound Brailler and a cane about one meter long. The more I grow, the bigger the cane. My friends are very helpful, and I can trust them. I can climb on the bars at recess. I can do anything I want if I try. You see, being blind doesn't mean a thing. Just because I may mess up on something doesn't mean it's the end of the world. I could always try again. And I don't need much help on things, either. Now you know what it's like being blind.

I WAS A YOUNG MOTHER BEING STIFLED BY BLINDNESS

by Barbara Pierce

Wife of a college professor, mother of three children, career woman, civic leader—all of these terms apply to Barbara Pierce, the President of the National Federation of the Blind of Ohio. She did not achieve the poise and self-confidence that she possesses today without going through a period of soul-searching and doubt. The National Federation of the Blind was a key factor in helping her find her way. So were her own introspection and self-analysis. Here is how she remembers it.

In 1973 I was twenty-eight years old and a faculty wife living in a small midwestern town with my loving husband and three small children.

Barbara Pierce as a young mother.

The main complication in my life was my blindness. My vision had deteriorated since childhood, and even though I had been introduced to Braille and the white cane as a teenager, I could still use my vision for some things, so I told myself I was not really blind. Since college, though, I had had to admit that my eyes now provided me with almost no useful information except which lights were on.

Despite the profound handicap of vision loss, I grew up in a happy family with a younger brother who was understanding of the extra time my parents spent working with me. They were truly amazing people.

Dad was easy-going and positive. Lots of homework? No problem; we'd dig our way through it—no regret at sacrificing his quiet evening. As an engineer he had no difficulty with the science and math, but German and diagramming sentences presented challenges to us both.

In the fifties there was little academic support for families whose blind children attended public schools. We were on our own to devise alternative methods of doing my work. So I diagrammed sentences in the air for Dad to transcribe onto paper and learned to do complex algebra in my head.

My mother was far more distressed about my blindness. Being a mother, she worried. Having an active conscience, she wondered if she were somehow responsible for my condition. I was dimly aware of her pain, but she never let it stand in the way of my growing up.

I went camping with the Girl Scouts, learned to cook and iron, and did my share of household chores. She never communicated her anxiety about my safety. She taught me about colors, make-up, and doing my hair. She saw to it that I learned to dress appropriately even though I couldn't tell what other people were wearing, and she suffered with me when the boys I liked ignored me or treated me like a sister. My senior year she first rejoiced with me and then began worrying again when I fell in love.

Thanks to my parents' support, I graduated second in my suburban high school class. I entered Oberlin College the following September and for the first time in my life had to face the prospect of getting my work done without a full-time reader/secretary at my disposal.

I learned quickly about hiring and supervising readers, and I worked hard. But I played hard too, taking part in college organizations and dating, though my heart was still entangled with my high school flame, attending a college far away.

The college campus was small and easy to memorize. I used a folding cane that I could make vanish whenever someone presented her (or preferably) himself to walk with me to my destination. I wouldn't allow friends to go out of their way for me, so I often didn't do social things or run errands I would have wanted to because I couldn't find anyone who was going that direction.

All that changed my senior year when I began to date one of my professors. It was one of those whirlwind romances that are the talk of small, close-knit communities. I graduated from Oberlin with high honors in June and became a faculty wife that September. I felt like a fairy-tale princess.

By 1973 Bob and I had bought a thirteen-room house that had originally been a dormitory. It was close enough to campus for him to walk to his office and for me to walk downtown and to the pediatrician, where I was going frequently by this time because we had three children: Steven, five; Anne, two; and Margaret, born two months prematurely that August.

The things I was doing I could do well. My children were happy, my home was as orderly as any with three small children, my husband's classes met often in our living room and ate home-baked cookies.

But I was beginning to feel that my life was much more restricted than I wanted it to be. I could not drive. I could not read print. I couldn't even read Braille very well because no one had ever encouraged me to work on building my reading speed when I was young. I hated my cane and used it as little as possible. It seemed to shriek to people of my blindness, and everyone knew that blind people couldn't do much. They made brooms in sheltered workshops or tuned pianos. They stood on street corners and sold pencils or, if they were musical, played the accordion. I was not like that.

But what was I like? What could I do with myself? It was a question that I could put off a little longer because the children were still small enough for me to pretend that I didn't yet want to go back to work.

Never during my struggles did I consider that other blind people might be able to help me. Everyone had always told me that I was not like other blind people. Since I had never known a blind person, I assumed that my friends and family were right. I told myself that I was really a sighted person who couldn't see. I was normal, and nothing that blind people could say would have much relevance to me because, even though my world was limited to the distance I could walk and the information I could glean from my recorded books and what my dear husband had time to read to me, I was not a shuffling, passive, doggedly cheerful blind puppet to be dragged around and handed whatever other people no longer wanted.

Then, in January of 1974, someone brought me a stack of recordings produced by the National Federation of the Blind. He said I might be interested in listening to them. I smiled politely and put them aside with no intention of wasting my time on such twaddle. But very soon thereafter my husband had to be away for a weekend, and the baby came down with her first cold. To complete my misery, I had read and returned every one of the recorded books lent to me by the National Library Service for the blind and Physically Handicapped. I faced the prospect of two days of walking a fussy baby and talking to two toddlers while having nothing to read. I remembered the stack of records and decided that they were better than nothing.

When Bob came home Sunday afternoon, expecting to find a frantic, ill-tempered wife, he found instead a woman who had been transformed. Poor man, he had to listen to the pent-up flood of discoveries that I had made. He is patient, and he paid close attention as I explained that I had discovered fifty thousand people who believed that blindness didn't have to consign one to poverty and helplessness. I had learned that as a member of the general public, I had been brainwashed like everyone else about blindness. I realized that my dislike of my cane was really rejection and denial of blindness. I had been working hard at doing things as well as sighted people not because blindness need not be more than a nuisance in my life, but because I didn't want anyone to think of me as blind. Dimly I had begun to understand that if I were ever to step beyond the confines of my current narrow life, it would be because I had come to terms with myself as I was—a blind woman with energy and dreams and the capacity to fulfill them.

No profound insight can remake a person overnight, but it is accurate to say that from then on I was a different person. I organized a local chapter of the Federation in my county. As I did so, I discovered that I could help other blind people who hadn't yet learned even the little I knew about coming to accept themselves and being proud of who they were. I also discovered just how many blind people had suffered real discrimination at society's hands.

I learned that I have been incredibly lucky. No one had tried to take my children away from me because I was a blind parent. This still happens to blind parents today despite the overwhelming evidence that blindness does not prevent a person from being a good parent.

Each time I have looked for a job, I have found one. I learned that blind people face a 70% unemployment rate—not because only 30% of us are capable to holding down good jobs, but because employers don't believe that we can.

As I became active in the National Federation of the Blind, I met blind people who simply did not recognize the boundaries I had always lived with. They traveled all over the country and the world independently, getting to their planes, retrieving their luggage, and coping with ground transportation without thinking twice about the task.

I discovered that I could do these things as well, and I cannot express the sensation of freedom I had packing for a plane trip and feeling no anxiety about the logistics of getting where I needed to go.

I discovered blind people who read Braille at 400 words a minute. Though I had been cheated as a child by not being forced to master the Braille code thoroughly, I could begin as an adult to change the situation.

The Federation also gave me personal fulfillment and a circle of wonderful friends who knew and loved me for who I was. I had work to do.

I learned new skills. As a result of these new skills and the self-confidence I have learned from the National Federation of the Blind, I applied for a job as a college administrator at Oberlin and got it. There I had a chance to educate many people about the abilities of the blind. I also had plenty of opportunities to learn to juggle husband, children, home, full-time job, and volunteer work.

I have moved on now to magazine editing. My children are almost grown, and my new job requires that I travel frequently. I can hardly remember the days when airports made my stomach turn inside out. Blindness is one of the characteristics that define me. It means that I can't drive a car or read print. It also means that I am organized and have a well-trained mind—two characteristics that most of my friends would give a great deal to possess.

I still have room to grow. None of us has ever become all that we can. I frequently discover little pockets of cowardice and insecurity in myself, but by and large, I am free thanks to the National Federation of the Blind.

MY JOURNEY INTO BLINDNESS

by Claire McCuller

Claire McCuller became a student at the Louisiana Center for the Blind, the training center for blind adults run by the National Federation of the Blind of Louisiana. She is a talented and sensitive elementary school teacher. When she began to lose her sight, her common sense told her that there were ways to combat her blindness. Here is her description of her struggle to find the answers she was seeking.

My journey into blindness began in 1979 when I was diagnosed as having Retinitis Pigmentosa (RP). The diagnosis itself was somewhat difficult to obtain. After I had repeatedly asked my ophthalmologist for an explanation of my inability to see things in my apartment that I knew were there, he finally asked me, "How many fingers am I holding up?" When I answered that I couldn't see his hand, much less his fingers, my journey began.

After tests, consultations, and large expenditures of money, I knew for certain that I was going to be blind though no one could tell me exactly when or how rapidly my loss of eyesight would occur. Furthermore, those people who consented to discuss the problem with me could not (or would not) tell me about options or advise me about what I should do next. A friend told me that there were agencies in the area that worked with the blind and suggested that I might receive support and services from them.

I made the necessary contacts, and one afternoon a counselor came to see me. The first thing he told me was that all blind people were retarded. In a few carefully chosen words (that I shall not repeat in this article) I told him that someone had messed up profoundly since I had just received my master's degree in educational administration. The meeting was quickly terminated.

Apparently wishing to make amends, the counselor called inviting me to come in and review the career file available in his office. On my arrival he suggested that I review the information about appropriate jobs available in the area. He especially advised me to look at the employment file card entitled "Baker's Assistant." Another meeting was quickly terminated.

Even at this time I recognized that, as my sight worsened, I would eventually need to learn new skills and have to make changes in my life. I wanted someone to tell me what those changes should be and how to implement them. Unfortunately it seemed that, no matter where I turned, no one was able to give me the information that I was seeking.

For the next eight years I continued in my search for an intelligent solution and a rational approach to my problems. Along the way I wrote letters to people who were supposed to know about rehabilitation and blindness, and I gathered and read information about as many different options as I could. My journey was mostly along dead-end paths.

As a finalist in Louisiana's Elementary Teacher of the Year contest, I had the pleasure of appearing on local television with my students. One of the questions the reporter asked me was "What are your goals and plans for the future?" I responded that because of the progression of my eye disease, I did not know how much longer I could remain in the regular classroom.

Enter Joanne Wilson, President of the National Federation of the Blind of Louisiana, and the staff at the Louisiana Center for the Blind. I received information from the Center after the broadcast of my television interview. And I immediately wrote a letter to Mrs. Wilson, who serves as director of the National Federation of the Blind's Center in Louisiana, expressing eight years' worth of uncertainty and frustration. She then called me at home. After talking to her, I realized that my journey into blindness had not come to a dead end; rather, it was about to take me to a smooth highway leading to useful information and intelligent solutions.

At the time of this writing I have been at the Center in Ruston, Louisiana, for two months. In this short time I have begun my study of Braille and computers and have become a more accurate typist. I am gradually overcoming my fear of travel under sleep shades using a white cane.

I have been introduced to the National Federation of the Blind and have adopted its philosophy as my own. However, perhaps the best education I have received at the Center has come from my observation of successful blind individuals associated with the Center. As I return to my teaching career this coming fall, my renewed self-confidence is allowing me to pursue new challenges in the field of education. I have decided to teach seventh and eighth grade gifted students in a new school rather than the fourth graders I have been teaching. My journey into blindness has not been without its bumps and detours, but now I can say that through my own persistence and curiosity and through the support I have received from the National Federation of the Blind at the Louisiana Center for the Blind, my journey continues in a positive direction.

ON EMPTYING WASTEBASKETS

by Catherine Horn Randall

Catherine Horn Randall is First Vice-President of the National Federation of the Blind of Illinois. She believes that blind children should be expected to meet responsibilities as well as receive favors. She knows from first-hand experience in her own childhood. Today she is a prominent civic and political leader in her hometown of Jacksonville, Illinois. Here is what she says:

An article I read in the *Reader's Digest* made me stop and reexamine my carefree childhood. Research shows, the article points out, that adults have happier and more productive lives if they were required to share in household chores when they were children.

Catherine Horn Randall is a civic and community leader. She is shown here as a child sitting in a rocking chair.

According to the article, an eleven-year-old philosopher of the 1980s instructed his mother as follows: "You only need to know three things about kids. Don't hit them too much, don't yell at them too much, and don't do too much for them."

As a child during the dark ages of the 1950s, I was not expected to do regular chores at home. I emptied wastebaskets sometimes and made my bed occasionally, but I was not regularly expected to do these jobs or others as a contributing member of the family. Over the years I have asked my mother why she did not expect me to do chores at home, and her answer has invariably been that my school work took up most of the time. I then have to remind her that I did not start bringing home much homework until I was twelve. I feel it is a disservice to any child, and especially to a blind child, not to be expected to share family responsibilities along with everyone else. Just because a child or teenager happens to be partially or totally blind should not exempt him or her from learning to take responsibility.

When homework assignments became routine, I was expected to do them. I loved school and didn't mind working hard to complete assignments. The one area, therefore, in which I was expected by my parents to follow through, I did. But in life we must learn also to complete jobs we don't like. This is called living up to our responsibilities.

Blind children have the right to learn to become independent people. This means they need to know how to do every chore around a house competently. I did not know how to iron when I left home for college. I sent my blouses to a laundry service, and I took a lot of ribbing about it. So many things in life would have been so much easier if I had learned to do them as a child or as a teenager.

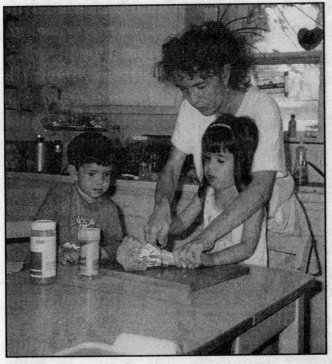

Emptying wastebaskets or cutting broccoli—there is no substitute for learning responsibilities as a child.

Diane Starin.

A WOMAN ON HORSEBACK

by Diane Starin

Diane Starin fell in love with horses when she was a little girl at a carnival. It was a love she didn't outgrow, despite the fact that her counselor called her desire to work with horses a pipe dream. Today she trains horses, teaches riding, and sharpens sheep shears to make ends meet. Here is her story.

Horses are interesting critters. They definitely have minds of their own. I have liked the animal since the time I was put on one at a carnival by my mother. I think it took her a couple hours to get me off. I hate to think how much that cost her. When I got to be about twelve years old, I decided that I had found the horse I had to have. The horse was starving and

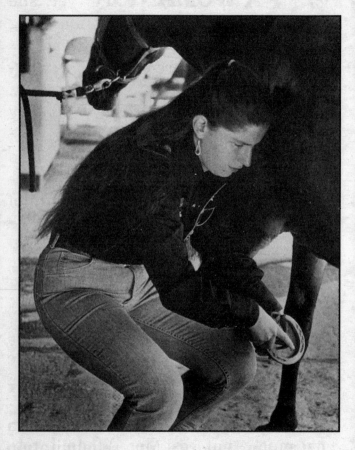

Diane Starin cares for her horses.

skinny. My mother was really afraid for me to own a horse and, yet, she wasn't one to hold me back from doing anything I wanted to do.

I think she figured this poor starving animal couldn't hurt me anyway. So the critter was purchased for fifty dollars. All kids like to race horses, and I was no exception. My horse turned into a fat, sleek, shiny runaway. When you grabbed a handful of mane and jumped on you needed to be ready to go, because he was a half mile down the road in about 30 seconds.

Later I purchased another neglected horse and raised her. She is fifteen years old now, and I still have her.

When I finished high school I decided to go to college and major in horse husbandry. My rehabilitation counselor said he knew a lot of blind people who had a lot of crazy pipe dreams and that I should figure out something that I could really do and get back to reality. I told him that it didn't really matter what he thought because I was going to go take that major anyway. He told me that if I did I wouldn't get any help from the state program for the blind. But I wasn't about to let the government run my life. So I applied for and won a scholarship from the National Federation of the Blind and one from Sierra College. I ended up with a degree in suburban agriculture and a certificate in horse husbandry.

While most people were running around getting readers, I was looking for trucks and horse trailers and such so that I could get to class. One of the classes was a hands-on horse training class. I had a horse trailer, and I met a friend who had a horse and a truck but no trailer. So between the two of us we had what we needed and off we went to class.

The instructor had definitely never seen a blind person before, not to mention having one in his horse training class. But he didn't seem particularly bothered about it. We agreed that we would figure out together how it could be done. I was lucky and pleased that he had that attitude.

At this point I was still a novice, and I did a lot of dumb things that you are not supposed to do with horses, but I learned. When you are training a young horse, you first do what is called ground work. The horse must be exercised and taught to obey before it is ready to be ridden. One of the things done in ground work is called lunging. It is done on a long line of about twenty feet, and you have the horse go around you in a circle. The arena had very, very soft footing, and it was difficult for me to hear the horse in the soft footing twenty feet away with all the other class members doing the same things with their horses.

I decided to take a leather thong with a little bell on it, like a sleigh bell or the kind you have on your Christmas tree, and tie one bell on a front leg and one on the opposite hind leg. Then, when I asked the horse to trot I could hear the second he started to do it. That was one of my alternative techniques for getting the horse to respond to me immediately. In horseback riding there is rarely anything that you ever do with the animal where you are not in contact with it. So for a blind person it is a much simpler task than it might seem because you either have contact directly through reins or through a rope, and you learn quickly what the horse is doing by what is coming to you through that rope or reins.

When you are riding it is something like typing. You are not supposed to look when you type. Likewise, when you ride a horse, and become more expert at it, you learn to feel your horse under you. This is not unique to blind people. All people who show and train horses don't need to look at the horse to know what it is doing. When I ride along I listen for the echoes from fences and posts in order to judge distance.

After I finished college, I bought a stallion and went into the breeding business. I didn't have any trouble developing techniques to use here either. I use sound a lot and believe me, when you are handling a stallion and someone is handling a mare, there is no trouble knowing where they are or which end you might be approaching.

I asked the California State Fair Manager about starting a therapeutic riding school on the fairgrounds. About a month later he called up and offered me a job managing the Sacramento Valley Polo Club. When I went down for my interview, the man who was the president of the club said that I had to demonstrate to him that I could clean a stall. This job didn't pay much, but I badly wanted that experience on my resume, so I took it. I thought it was interesting that he wanted to see if I could clean a stall, but it never occurred to him to ask me something important like how I would get the horses to the track a half a mile away. The track was a one mile, standard regulation race track, and I was to gallop the club's four horses three miles each and everyday to keep them in shape. I decided that after I had been galloping around this track three times that I might want to be able to find the gate and get off of there. The simplest thought that occurred to me was to leave a transistor radio playing at the gate post.

In addition to caring for the horses, I had to baby-sit the people who were members of the Polo Club. I'd saddle up for them and talk to them. I had to ride with the ones who didn't want to ride alone. By the way, when I finally quit the Polo Club I had ten horses under my care and I was still getting the same pay. But I got the experience on my resume.

I am currently giving horseback riding lessons in my local area. I will always have horses because they are my passion, but now I am moving into a new small business, which I operate out of my home. It is a clipper blade sharpening business. Sheep shearers use a lot of blades.

The way I got started into this was quite by accident. I had moved to a small town, and I needed to get my clipper blades sharpened. I asked the barber, and the dog groomer, and the beautician—where do you send your clipper blades? They said, we either take them to Sacramento, or we mail them back east. I thought, that is ridiculous! It's a three-minute process. All I have to do is buy the machine. I could do it out of my home with no overhead, no inventory, and no extra utilities.

About that time I was listening to a local swap shop program and, low and behold—a one-in-a-million chance—there was a used clipper blade sharpening machine on swap shop. I called up the person in Sacramento who had sharpened my clipper blades for years. I said, "What kind of machine don't I want to buy? I don't know anything about them." He said, "If the wheel is fourteen inches across you are in business." Well, it was wider than that across, and I went down to the lady and bought it from her for half price.

She had only used it four times. She said that she couldn't make it work and that she would be my first customer if I could get it going. I found there wasn't much to it. You turn the machine on, and it spins the wheel at 700 rpms. After you powder and oil

the wheel, you put the blade which
you hold with a block of wood at a certain angle and go from edge to middle
and back from middle to edge for five
seconds and you are finished. So for
three dollars for two minutes work, it's
not a bad deal. I sharpen clipper
blades for money so that I can train
horses for love. It's a combination that
works for me, and my blindness really
has nothing to do with it.

IS THERE SHAME?

by Jan Kafton

When a sensitive woman, who happens to be blind, meets repeated rejection in her attempts to lead a normal, full life, what impact does it have on her? What does she do? What <u>should</u> she do? Jan Kafton tells us. Here is what she has to say.

There have been only a few events in my life which have had a tremendous impact on me. The most recent of these events occurred in March of 1988. This experience resulted in marriage.

However, even more importantly, I was forced to re-evaluate my personal view of my own blindness. The circumstances and my thought processes merit an explanation.

For several months I had been using a dating service called Selective

Introductions. This service involves calling a pay phone number which presents messages from men in a chosen age group. Then one has the opportunity to record a message, including the phone number.

There were quite a few men I had met who were indeed friendly, courteous, and fun. Yet, there were a few of them who could not handle my blindness at all. In fact, one or two of them actually left after they had arrived and met me.

In most cases I did not mention my blindness over the phone when the initial contact was made. Not one of the men had dated me more than twice, and my discouragement mounted a great deal.

On a Tuesday evening I received a call from an extremely personable, friendly young man, and we talked for a few minutes. I discovered that his background was very similar to mine. We shared a lot of common interests, including music, literature, and other recreational activities. Also, we are both musicians.

At any rate we decided to meet and have dinner together that same night. Just before the end of the conversation I said to him that I thought he should know one more important item regarding me. I told him that I had a visual problem. He then asked me what that meant. I said that I had no sight.

In every other instance I have always said that I was blind, without any hesitation. What caused my unwillingness to say that I was blind? Lon's response to my statement brought me up short. He simply said, "So what?"

Yes, I did meet Lon that Tuesday night, and the rest is history. He has continually confirmed what I already knew to be true for me, that my blindness has been reduced to a physical nuisance. He is entirely supportive of that viewpoint and of my goal to be successful in life.

As blind people, we do face many problems. Yet, that is why there is a National Federation of the Blind, which is always available for encouragement and collective action if necessary.

Many have led the way for our present progress and future first-class citizenship as blind persons. I not only owe a great deal to each of them, but I do owe a lot to my husband, Lon Kafton. He allowed me to look at my blindness and helped me to know there is indeed no shame in being blind. I choose to go on productively and proudly.

I WANT THAT

By Peggy Pinder

Many things can happen when a teenager suddenly loses her sight. What <u>does</u> happen depends on a variety of unpredictable factors—family influence, teachers, chance. Perhaps for each person there is a crucial incident which changes everything that comes after. Peggy Pinder believes this to be true for her.

As you read her story keep in mind that the teenager you're reading about went on to finish high school, earn a bachelor's degree with double majors in history and philosophy at Cornell College, Mount Vernon, Iowa (where she reported for and then was chief editor of the college newspaper); earn a law degree from Yale, serve five years as a state criminal prosecutor, and establish a private law practice in which she now works. Here in her own words is what happened.

I lost my sight as a teenager.

Because of my eye condition my eventual total blindness was predictable. Even so, nobody had ever told me or my parents that this could happen. I was devastated.

I had been to the store earlier in the day. While waiting at the checkout counter I had picked up a magazine as one does to pass the time. I read little bits of it, and it looked interesting—so I bought it.

Later that day at home I picked up the magazine. And, that was how I found out I was blind. I couldn't read it at all.

I remember wondering if I should tell my mother who was in the kitchen because I could guess what trouble would start. I remember thinking about it and deciding to tell her because, sooner or later, people would notice that I was not reading anything. That would include schoolwork which would be troublesome, too. So, I sighed and told my mother. I was sure right about the trouble.

I was totally unprepared for such a change. I didn't know it was coming. I had no techniques like Braille or a white cane with which to continue my life. I didn't want such techniques anyway because that would mean that I would always be blind and, as I thought then, unable to do anything with my life.

Adding this horrifying and unexpected change to the other changes of adolescence was just too much for me. I withdrew into myself. Nobody understood how bad it really was. There was no one to whom I could talk, nobody who understood. They all said things would work out, but they could all see. What did they know?

During this time, I happened to hear some blind people on the radio one night. They were in town for a convention, they said. They explained to the radio audience that blindness was not the horrible tragedy that everyone thinks it is. They were blind themselves, and they all held jobs, had families, went where they wanted.

They said blindness was not a tragedy—that it all centered around how you handled it, just like hundreds of other differences among people that we all deal with every day—like being too short to reach a cupboard or too light to carry heavy loads. That's why we have stepstools and carts.

According to them blindness was no different. You just had to figure out ways to do things others do with sight. The ways exist. Blindness could be reduced to the level of a nuisance.

I turned off the radio. It made me mad to hear people talking such nonsense. I knew how bad it was to be blind. I could tell them a thing or two.

And, how dare they say that I could lead a full life as a blind person?

I hated people who tried to sugar-coat things and act like nothing was wrong when obviously everything was. They were blind. Why didn't they just shut up and accept their limitations gracefully as I was doing?

My way of accepting my limitations was to become a bookworm. Books are put into Braille or recorded onto tapes and distributed to blind people through a nationwide library system. I read everything. I had always been a reader. My whole family is. That was one of the most devastating things about blindness. I couldn't just pick up what others were reading and read it.

Even so, there were things I could read, and I read all the time. I turned down invitations and declined to do things because I had some reading to do. It is not good for a teenager to spend the years just before adulthood in her room reading during the time when everyone else is learning to take more and more responsibility and to interact personally with the world around her.

But that's what I did. I didn't know what else to do. I found contact with other people uncomfortable. They were uncomfortable because they "didn't know how to act around a blind person," as they put it. Why couldn't I just be a person anymore? I was now some strange being who upset people. That upset me. It upset me all the more because I agreed with them. I didn't know how to act around me either. So I read books and lived in the lives of other people.

My system worked through most of high school. But it wouldn't work after that. My parents weren't willing to let me continue to hide out from the world. They knew that there were blind people who worked, who took responsibility, who made lives for themselves. They were determined to have that chance for me. They began searching.

I well remember the exact moment and the exact location when I discovered that my parents were right. I was standing in a hallway, waiting my turn to speak to the occupant of the office beside which I was standing, doing nothing in particular.

I heard someone down the hall and around the corner come out of an office. I heard him lock his door with a key and check to be sure the door was locked. I then heard him walk briskly down the hall, turn the corner into the hall where I stood, walk by me, and go out of the door at the other end of the hall.

I knew he was blind because I heard his white cane. I was stunned! Simple tasks? Yes. But I couldn't get over that here was a blind person making his own schedule, caring for his and his employer's property responsibly, determining where he would go, deciding how to get there, and then doing it. I couldn't do any of those things for myself. Not really.

Or, could I? He had. If he had, then maybe I could, too. He was blind. That hadn't stopped him. Maybe, just maybe. I remember straightening up from my relaxed posture against the wall and saying the words very clearly in my mind: "I want <u>that</u>."

You couldn't tell me in mere words about blind people doing things. You couldn't talk at me over the radio. You couldn't give me stories to read about the blind. It didn't work. I didn't believe it. But it turned out that all you really had to do was to put one blind person in front of me, managing tasks I thought were impossible with ease and style, and I could get the point. I could do it, too.

I found that blind person who had walked by me in the hall and found out how he had found the self-confidence I thought was impossible for me. He is still a friend of mine and a colleague in the organization to which he introduced me, the National Federation of the Blind. Incidentally, I learned later that he was one of the very people I had heard on the radio program that had made me so angry years before.

Through the National Federation of the Blind I met blind people from all walks of life—young and old, wealthy and poor, well-educated and with little schooling, technically skilled and unskilled. I met a whole cross section of American society with the one common thread that they are blind.

Meeting all these people reinforced the original intuition I had had when I observed my friend walk down the hall. Regardless of their backgrounds, all these blind people were managing their own lives. If they could do it so could I.

Going to meetings and national conventions of the National Federation of the Blind showed me in a different way the same thing that the guy walking down the hall had first demonstrated: that blind people have only one thing in common, blindness. But they must consciously take that blindness and examine it, understand what it is, understand how it functions in the world around them.

Until blindness is understood, you can just end up in your room, reading, avoiding the whole thing. Once blindness is understood, then the whole rest of your life opens up.

I became a member of the National Federation of the Blind after learning these things. Two things drew me into the organization. One was that I need the continuing support and encouragement of other blind people who keep reminding me that the only limitations on me are the ones I impose upon myself.

The second and equally important reason was that I was so very lucky.

I had parents who believed in my future and set about helping me to find it. We found self-confident, capable blind people in the National Federation of the Blind, organized and ready to help others.

I want to be sure that all other blind people have that same chance. Blindness was devastating to me because I didn't understand it and thought it had ended my useful life at thirteen.

Some day, through the work of the National Federation of the Blind, I hope that all my fellow countrymen will have the basic understanding that my parents had gained from their brief contacts with self-confident blind people. Because it was that understanding that blind people <u>could</u> have productive lives that kept my parents searching for help when I was a teenager.

The National Federation of the Blind was there for me when I needed it. That's why I'll continue to work in it: for my own growth and protection and to insure that the same will be there for every other blind person.

CONFESSIONS OF A SCHOLARSHIP WINNER

by Jennifer Lehman

Jennifer Lehman is a sophomore at St. Norbert College, majoring in Communications. She won an NFB scholarship which brought with it the chance to attend our National Convention—perhaps the most valuable part of her scholarship. Here is how she tells it:

As I stepped from the oppressively humid jetway into the startling coolness of the New Orleans airport, I felt the apprehension I had been fighting to control begin to overwhelm me. Flying alone for the first time, I had just arrived in an unfamiliar city to spend a week attending a convention of a group about which I knew almost nothing. Lurking beneath my apprehension, however, was a spark of excitement. I realized that this trip could be a challenging and fun adventure. I could not have known then how much I would learn and what an exciting and unforgettable experience the annual convention of the National Federation of the Blind would be.

Prior to this convention my contact with other blind people had been limited. I was the first blind student to enter the Watertown public school system and am presently the only one at St. Norbert College. Apart from my younger sister, many of the blind people I had met seemed to exemplify the stereotypic image of blindness. They seemed totally dependent upon others to meet all of their needs. I was not anxious to spend a week surrounded by such people. I felt that there were no other blind people like my sister and me—people who thought of their blindness, not as a handicap or an insurmountable hurdle, but as something which, though sometimes a nuisance, did not have to keep them from doing what they wanted to do with their lives.

Soon after arriving at the convention, I discovered, to my relief, that I had been wrong. I was among people whose attitudes and accomplishments I admired and who reached out and made me feel that I was a part of their huge family. The sense of community I felt was one of the most positive aspects of the convention for me.

Another positive aspect was the chance to learn more about the NFB. Before this trip I knew almost nothing about the group. Through conversations with members and many excellent speeches, I learned a great deal about the beliefs and actions of the National Federation of the Blind. I plan to become an active member and may even work to start a student division in Wisconsin.

The convention taught me as much about myself as it did about the NFB.

I have always considered myself fairly independent, but this convention taught me to be even more so as an improved cane traveler. Walking with so many other people who were also using canes, I gained new skills as well as more of the confidence I needed to help me travel better. As I relaxed and opened up to people, I also gained much-needed self-confidence. I hope that the positive effects this convention had on my self-image will last a lifetime.

Attending the annual convention of the National Federation of the Blind is an event I will never forget. I am extremely grateful to the members of the scholarship committee and all those who worked to make this experience possible for me. By winning the Wisconsin NFB scholarship, I received more than just the money to help pay for my tuition. I gained confidence, knowledge, friends, and memories which I will cherish forever.

HAMBURGERS AND THE PRACTICE OF LAW

by Marc Maurer

Twenty-five years ago Marc Maurer was a blind teenager, unsure of himself and wondering what he could do. Today he is a successfully practicing lawyer—with a home, a wife, two well-adjusted, active children, and a full life. He is also the President of the National Federation of the Blind, the organization which helped him set his values and start on the road to success. Here is what he says about how he found himself and what it was like to wonder if he as a blind person could have a dream and hope for tomorrow.

It seems to me that development of life stops when the dreams go away. It isn't that a person dies; instead, the interesting part of existence is all in the past. When there are no dreams

Marc Maurer cooks hamburgers on the charcoal.

for a bright tomorrow, hope itself withers and fades.

These reflections brought fear and agonizing uncertainty to me when I was a junior in high school. Blind kids (I was then, as I am today, totally blind) were expected to attend grade school and high school. Some went on to college. Many did not. My high school buddies (all sighted) were planning for the future. Some intended to get college degrees; some planned to enter the local business community; some wanted to gain a technical education directed toward the trades; some preferred farming. I was afraid that none of these choices was available to me.

On a warm evening in the early spring of that year, I sat by the window listening to the night sounds and wondering what was in store for me. Except for the teachers at the school for the blind, which I had attended through the fifth grade, I had met only one blind adult. He sold pencils in front of the Ben Franklin store in my home town. He was a silent man, who seemed to me to be elderly and gloomy. I hoped fervently that I would not be like him. But who could I be like? What could I do that would be worth remembering? More to the point, what could I do to make a living? Would I ever be able to travel, to visit interesting places, to see the world? I knew about (or thought I knew about) hundreds of things that blind people could not do.

The magic age of sixteen meant (for the sighted) that three things happened: first, the sixteen-year-old got a driver's license; second, dating was permitted; and third, real work became available—construction jobs, factory work, retailing and warehouse assignments—the kind of employment with a forty or forty-eight-hour week, a time clock to be punched, and a regular paycheck. Sixteen meant the possibility of freedom and money, but that is not what sixteen meant for me. I was to learn from personal experience that I, a blind person, could not get a job in the factory, and the driver's license was out of the question. The symbols of coming adulthood were not mine.

As I pondered the question of the future, sitting beside the window and listening to the creatures of the night, I reflected upon the odd jobs I had done to bring in a little pocket money. In addition to shoveling snow and raking leaves, I had put a roof on a garage, performed some minor concrete work, washed cars, set up a lawn-mowing business, and operated a tiny manufacturing company. My father had some woodworking equipment in the basement of our house. I liked the machinery. It seemed to me that although others might not want to hire me, I might be able to start a cabinet-making business, which would bring me at least some money. Of all of the choices that I thought might be available, this seemed to me to be the best—and even it seemed doubtful.

It was not exactly what I would have chosen for my life. Woodworking was a satisfying thing to do, but there were other things that were far more exciting.

One of them was politics. The mayor of my town had, while I was a junior in high school, awarded a contract for the construction of a public facility. The award did not go to the low bidder. I wanted this situation investigated. I called the mayor and asked him to come to my civics class to explain why he had spent public money which could have been saved if he had given the contract to the person who had bid the lowest amount. When the mayor appeared, I was so astonished that I couldn't ask him all the mean questions I had planned.

I was also interested in inventions and mechanics. One day I devised a scheme. A battery could be used to turn an electrical motor. The electric motor could be used to drive a generator. The generator could be used to charge the battery. The system could be built so that it would never need any additional power. Some grown-ups laughed at me, saying that my idea was a perpetual motion machine which obviously could not work. They never told me why it wouldn't work, and I could not understand why they laughed. Years later I learned what a perpetual motion machine is and why the notion is impractical.

Although my hopes for a self-contained electrical system had been dashed, I was still fascinated with machinery. Maintaining the family lawn mower, repairing door latches, replacing the washers in faucets, doing the minor repairs on our 1954 Plymouth, and similar tasks were my responsibility at home. I bought old lawn mower engines so I could take them to pieces to find out how they worked. I used the same process on everything else mechanical that my mother and father hadn't told me I couldn't touch.

But there were also the academic interests: physics, chemistry, mathematics, English, and Latin. The Latin class was usually about war or high adventure—about how the Romans conquered the known world, or about the adventures of Aeneus traveling from Troy to establish the city of Rome.

I wondered if there would be any high adventure for me. Defense of my country in military service seemed out of the question; international relations were only an exciting dream; and the intrigue and masterful dealing of business were also (as I imagined then) quite impossible. Would I ever step beyond the boundaries of a small midwestern town? What realistic dreams for a bright future could be mine? I picked the best I knew—not politics, not international relations, not business, not scientific discovery. I decided to be a cabinet-maker.

Later that spring I received an unexpected telephone call at school. Such a thing had never happened to me until that time. Telephone calls for students were rare, and nobody was ever excused from class to take one. A man from the National Federation of the Blind was urging me to consider attending college. He told me that I should take the Scholastic Aptitude Test, and he said that he would help to arrange matters so that I could. I was dumbfounded. I didn't know how he knew I existed. But I was also delighted, flattered, and a little scared. I wanted very much to go to college, but I wasn't sure I had the ability, and I didn't have the money. Even though

I wasn't sure what taking the test would mean, I agreed to do it.

When I arrived for the examination, I met other members of the National Federation of the Blind. I wasn't sure that I could take them seriously. They spoke about matriculation at college as though it were an everyday occurrence. They seemed to think that money could be found to meet the tuition payments and the living expenses, and they acted as if blind people could attend the best schools. They told me that the junior college in my home town was a good enough school, but that I might consider one of the major universities.

Within the next year I met the president of the National Federation of the Blind, Dr. Kenneth Jernigan. He told me to forget my chuckle-headed notions about being or expecting of myself less than the best, and he urged me to work as hard as I could to get ready for tough competition. "Perhaps," he said, "you can be a scientist, an engineer, a lawyer, or a diplomat, but you will never get the opportunity unless you have the willingness to work, the belief in yourself, and the ability to compete successfully. You must learn to work, and you must get a good education." He also demonstrated to me in a dramatic way that I was not considering all of the opportunities available to me—he taught me to barbecue hamburgers over a hot charcoal fire. First, we poured charcoal into the grill and doused it with lighter fluid. Then, he told me to strike a match and light the fire. Immediately, there was a substantial blaze as the fluid burned and ignited the charcoal. Presently, the fire settled down to a steady, intense heat. My teacher—Dr. Jernigan, a man as blind as I am—instructed me to put on a pair of welding gloves. He told me barbecuing would be no problem while I wore the gloves. They would protect me from the fire. He told me that I could put my hand directly into the blaze without being burned, and he invited me to do it. I wondered if he had lost his mind. Very cautiously, I reached toward the fire. He was quite right. I handled burgers and hot racks with my gloved hands. It was no problem at all. The burgers we cooked and ate were excellent, and so was the lesson. If I can do this, I thought, what else is possible?

With the help of the National Federation of the Blind, I studied for a bachelor's degree at the University of Notre Dame and for a law degree at Indiana University Law School. I passed the bar and became a lawyer. I learned that the things members of the National Federation of the Blind told me were true. Blind people can be a part of our society. Some of us practice law. If a client urgently needs the help of a lawyer, and if justice is on your side, the practice of law is one of

the most exciting jobs there is to do.
Blindness does not prevent planning
and working for a brighter tomorrow.
I did not imagine that I might stand
in the federal courts to address the ju-
diciary. But I followed the advice of my
blind friends who said: Don't let
yourself be limited in your aspira-
tions—dream big. We will help you
make it come true.

National Federation of the Blind

You can help us spread the word...

...about our Braille Readers Are Leaders contest for blind schoolchildren, a project which encourages blind children to achieve literacy through Braille.

...about our scholarships for deserving blind college students.

...about Job Opportunities for the Blind, a program that matches capable blind people with employers who need their skills.

...about where to turn for accurate information about blindness and the abilities of the blind.

Most importantly, you can help us by sharing what you've learned about blindness in these pages with your family and friends. If you know anyone who needs assistance with the problems of blindness, please write:

Marc Maurer, President
1800 Johnson Street, Suite 300
Baltimore, Maryland 21230-4998
Your contribution is tax-deductible.